Colorful Parrots

Tropical Birds Coloring Book

Magnificent Nature - Macaws, Cockatoos, Toucans In Forest

Rachel Mintz

Images used under license from Shutterstock.com

Join Our Coloring Books VIP Group
Members Get Giveaways, Deep Discount Offers,
Win Prizes – Visit Site To Join (It's Free)

www.ColoringBookHome.com

Thank you for coloring with us

Please consider to rate & review

More from our coloring books:

Beauty Garden

Rachel Mintz

Girls & Flowers Coloring Book

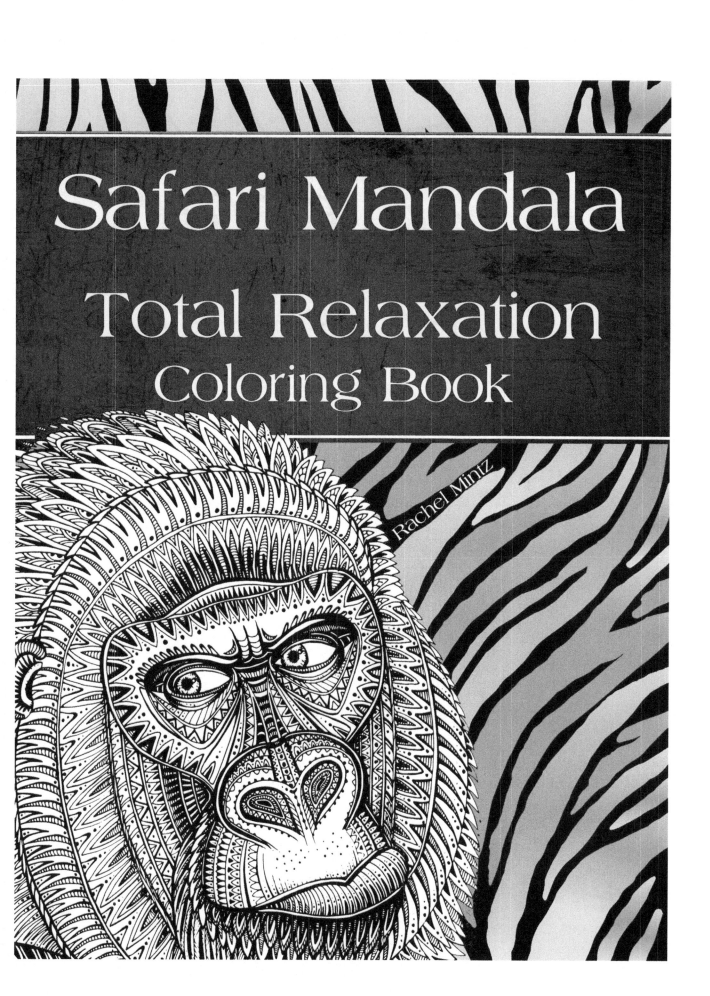

Join Our Coloring Books VIP Group
Members Get Giveaways, Deep Discount Offers,
Win Prizes – Visit Site To Join (It's Free)

www.ColoringBookHome.com

Thank you for coloring with us

Please consider to rate & review

Made in the USA
Las Vegas, NV
25 July 2021

27015478R00039